The Killer Handyman
WILLIAM PATRICK FYFE

Volume VII

by CL Swinney

The Killer Handyman
WILLIAM PATRICK FYFE
Volume VII
by CL Swinney

Crimes Canada

True Crimes That Shocked The Nation

www.CrimesCanada.com

ISBN-13: 978- 1517162412
ISBN-10: 1517162416

Copyright and Published (2015)

VP Publications an imprint of

RJ Parker Publishing, Inc.

Published in Canada

Copyrights

This book is licensed for your personal enjoyment only. This book may not be re-sold or given away to other people. If you would like to share this book with another person, please purchase an additional copy for each recipient. If you are reading this book and did not purchase it, or it was not purchased for your use only, then please return to the author and purchase your own copy. Thank you for respecting the hard work of the author. All rights reserved. No part of this publication can be reproduced or transmitted in any form or by any means without prior written authorization from Peter Vronsky or RJ Parker of VP Publications and RJ Parker Publishing, Inc. The unauthorized reproduction or distribution of a copyrighted work is illegal. Criminal copyright infringement, including infringement without monetary gain, is investigated by the FBI and is punishable by fines and federal imprisonment.

Enjoy these top rated true crime eBooks from VP Publications **FREE** as part of your Kindle Unlimited subscription. You can read it on your Kindle Fire, on a computer via Kindle Cloud Reader or on any smartphone with the free Kindle reading app.

View All True Crime and Crime Fiction Books by RJ Parker Publishing at the following Amazon Links:

[Amazon Kindle - USA](#)

[Amazon Kindle - Canada](#)

[Amazon Kindle - UK](#)

[Amazon Kindle - Australia](#)

Introduction

February 1955, and Toronto, Ontario, was experiencing the coldest month it would see the entire year. The brutal temperatures, averaging sixteen degrees Fahrenheit, kept residents inside their homes, huddled under blankets trying to remain warm. Many locals were still excited about the subway completion at the end of 1954, but they continued to grieve the loss of eighty-one citizens during Hurricane Hazel. Immigrants and newcomers from Atlantic Canada were moving to the area in record numbers, and the provincial government soon created the Municipality of Metropolitan Toronto. For the most part, times were relatively peaceful.

On the bitter cold morning of February 27, 1955, a male child was born to young parents in town. The baby's biological father disappeared, never to be heard from again, while the mother struggled to keep food on the table for her and the newborn. Somewhere along the line, the child's extended family intervened. About age three, the toddler wound up being raised by his aunt. Oddly, she too was reclusive. It's unclear why the boy's aunt raised him. Not much has ever been known about her.

When the child became a man, he frequently traveled, making it more difficult to obtain facts about various times in his life. Unfortunately, he chose the trodden path and committed petty crimes. Continuing unchecked, he became increasingly brazen and destructive… eventually committing rape and finally cold-blooded murder.

His name is William Patrick Fyfe, and he's the focus of this Crimes Canada book.

***

The status and names of his parents eluded me, despite months of investigation. In addition, specifics about the aunt proved equally elusive. William's childhood has remained a mystery to most people outside the circle of doctors who have tried to "cure" him (past and current), his aunt, and William himself. They are presumably the only ones who know what happened during his adolescence, what ultimately made him snap and become a serial killer. Speculation has shrouded what or why William Fyfe became "The Killer Handyman," but those questions are still unanswered.

His case enthralled me from the beginning. Countless months of research provided noteworthy information about his early adult life. Additional details became known about him once he began preying on female victims. The Fyfe story, and the stories about his victims, are important for Canada and, sadly, the truly sick and demented world of serial killers. The following is what's known about William Fyfe to date.

***

When William Fyfe was three (1958), he and his aunt moved to Montreal. The reason his mother turned over custody to the aunt has remained a mystery. As a law enforcement member, I've become familiar with cases where one or both parents either die or get arrested and therefore they cannot raise their child. Perhaps that was the case with William. His aunt became primary care provider until he reconnected with his mother well into adulthood, during his late thirties.

Many people have speculated that something terrible must have happened to him as a child while living with his aunt. Contradictory to that theory, though, "Billie's" aunt managed to instill in him admirable traits. Without further verification, we don't know if someone else in his life was responsible for that influence. For example, he remained in school, well into high school, and eventually became a successful handyman.

It's generally accepted knowledge that a child who's reared by a mother and father has a better chance of being properly socialized than one who isn't. I'm not saying single parents aren't amazing. For a period in my life, my mother raised me by herself, and I turned out decent. I possess a Bachelor's degree in sociology and have spoken to prominent sociologists and psychologists regarding socialization and the modern family. They all agree that having a mother and father is ideal. It is certainly easier to provide guidance, team discipline, financial support, and many of the other highly regarded socialization skills required to build a strong foundation for a child. Studies prove that chances are more likely for someone raised in a two-parent home to become a successful and a contributing member of society.

Somewhere during his formidable years, William Fyfe's wiring became crossed...to a point that his acts were no longer human, but more closely resembled that of a raging homicidal animal. Adding more peculiarity to this case, though, was the fact that William was actually capable of exhibiting "normal" behavior. However, within the blink of an eye, he would morph into a stone-cold, malicious killer and rapist.

Fyfe's adult life took a turn for the worse beginning most notably in 1977, at the age of twenty-two. According to newspaper articles and court documents, Fyfe was convicted of several charges including abduction, libel, theft, breaking and entering, and pretending to solemnize a marriage.

At the core of William's issues was a dependency on drugs. He would later seek counseling for his addiction, although it was never clear that he actually shook the habit but rather learned how to operate better under the influence. Some of his behavior could be explained and marginally understood if you considered he was under the influence most of the time. He managed to find and complete odd jobs in various provinces, mostly to make money to fuel his drug habit. If the jobs dried up, he'd resort to residential burglary. Tragically, he used that early experience to enhance his confidence and skills as he headed toward first-degree murder.

***

I've interviewed and arrested hundreds of drug users in my police career. The overwhelming majority of them commit property crimes to sell what they steal for cash, and usually those capers yield very small amounts, requiring multiple thefts to obtain enough cash to get high. Without counseling or family support, their demons begin to haunt them and appear at the most inopportune times. In addition, the more they use, the more tolerant their body becomes to the drug, requiring larger doses of narcotics to get high. It's a terrible cycle that rarely gets broken.

In the late 1970s, after Fyfe was released from jail for the above-noted cases, he became vagabond-like. He resided in St. Laurent, LaSalle, Verdun, and later Saint-Jerome in 1993. ([1])

At some point, between 1993 and 1999, he reunited with his biological mother and lived at her home, described as a makeshift barn. It was a structure situated behind the main home on property that belonged to another family, in Barrie, Canada.

In 1999, when this case burst wide open, that location would play a significant role in the investigation. The location also provided much greater insight as to who William Fyfe truly was. Interestingly enough, although court orders and documents were needed to obtain search warrants for the property, William's mother's name was omitted. That, in itself, wasn't odd because investigators have been known to do that. In this case, they obviously believed Fyfe's mother had no involvement in William's activities.

Unique in William Fyfe's upbringing was the fact that his childhood was so closely guarded and few true facts were ever revealed. Normally, volumes of information would have been printed and stored about a serial killer. Law enforcement personnel would have thoroughly investigated the suspect (and subsequently convicted criminal) in an effort to understand his motives, thoughts, and modus operandi (MO). Much of the information could have been used to help identify future killers or ferret out copy-cats. In addition, citizens have traditionally been fascinated with the deviancy and disturbing lifestyles of serial killers as evidenced by novels and stories written about these monsters.

We shake our heads, wondering how in the world they could do such things. Researchers, psychologists, police investigators, and I have combed what little data there is about William Fyfe's childhood looking for clues as to why he did what he did. More importantly, the question has always been, why did he become a monster?

Each of us was met with negative results. William Fyfe has also been interviewed numerous times as investigators attempted to shed light on his behavior, and again, they were unsuccessful at learning his motives. Only Fyfe himself will ever know what his childhood was like. Most serial killers have particularly disturbing childhoods and are typically physically and emotionally abused by one or both of their parents.

In this case, no one knows if that was William's fate. I believe he would not have reconnected with his mother and lived with her later in life if she had abused him as a child. Since he preyed on elderly women, I believe he would have killed his mother long ago if she had been the source of his abuse.

We'll later see that William, once apprehended, exhibited behaviors very inconsistent with other serial killers, adding further speculation about what happened inside his sick head. Unlike most serial killers, he did not seek publicity or notoriety based on his killing sprees and was quiet during his subsequent high-profile court case. In fact, he repeatedly tried to avoid any popularity associated with him, the murders he confessed to, or his well-known case. At one point, he fought for the right to be moved to a different prison to escape certain celebrity status he'd obtained in Montreal. He later won that fight, but only after he provided a statement regarding the brutal murders of five more women. A deal was struck with the prosecutor and the police department in which William was moved to the prison of his choice. That particular one had the exact same size cells as all the other prisons in Canada, but it had a psychiatric component that William's defense attorney noted his client needed.

Several reports and documents I read while researching this case indicated that William was married at one time and possibly fathered a child. However, no further documentation, such as a marriage license or birth certificate was available to confirm this. Still, according to Commander Andre Bouchard, who was the primary investigator for the William Fyfe case, he believed William's marriage might have lasted as long as four years. Very few details were available about his ex-wife or the possible child they had.

Upon finishing this story, you'll probably continue to ask yourself…as I do…if he does have an ex-wife and child, are they still alive?

Although it's heavily speculated that William exhibited odd tendencies and lived an abnormal lifestyle, no proof of that ever existed. In fact, the opposite appeared true. He basically lived "under the radar," and people who knew him described him as generous.

It's strange, at least to me, to hear a serial killer being described that way.

A few neighbors stated that William was full of community spirit, but also tended to preach to others about their weight gains or other socially unacceptable habits like drinking and smoking. I found this fascinating because William used drugs heavily and drank alcohol quite often. He smoked cigarettes regularly and was rumored to have many lovers. It seemed that William knew doing these things were bad for his health and mostly socially unacceptable and, therefore, wrong to do. But he continued smoking, drinking and using drugs, regardless. William certainly did not practice what he preached, but people generally seemed to get along with him.

What little is known about him seems more like most handymen I know, kind of rough around the edges, but basically harmless. That turns out not to be the case here.

***

William lived a rather simple life by most standards. He owned nothing really lavish. No prized possessions (that we know of). Fyfe was a capable painter, carpenter, builder of pools, and other basic construction occupations. Because of this, he naturally assumed the role of a handyman. People who used his services said he charged fair prices and did competent work. These stories indicated that William managed to function normally within society for long periods of time without a problem. Instead of helping solve the riddle of what made William tick, however, these facts only made the end result more unbelievable.

He primarily worked in Quebec, where he moved to seek treatment for his drug addiction. This point, at least in my opinion, demonstrated that William knew he had a problem and tried to do something to fix it. It showed that he was responsible and could make rational decisions. The program touched a spot in his heart because once he'd completed it, he remained associated with it and later became a counselor. He said he did so "because I enjoyed helping others like me."([2]) I prefer to believe he was talking about working with people who had drug addiction issues instead of people who shared similar serial killer ideations.

In reality, it doesn't matter what made William Fyfe tick, what his childhood was like, or who raised him. Sure, we'd love to know every single detail about him to attempt to wrap our minds around how he became a ruthless killer, but he's remained an anomaly due to the fact he flew under the radar for so long.

William began exhibiting socially unacceptable behavior in his twenties, resulting in numerous arrests and contacts with law enforcement. Shortly thereafter, and likely during his free time from incarceration, he developed a significant dependency on drugs and committed further crimes to fund his habit. It's possible he was properly socialized but suffered some psychotic breakdown or had his heart broken and later snapped. We'll later see that he maliciously stabbed his victims repeatedly and killed numerous women. He sexually violated most of his prey after they died at his hands. It was also possible that the euphoric rush he obtained while having sex with recently dead women was one reason he killed them.

Unless he has a change of heart and decides to open up about his life, we might never know much about him beyond what science, on-record statements, investigations, and his own admissions have already taught us.

The gaps in Fyfe's life timeline were significant and became a focal point in 1999 for the Montreal Police (MP) and the Ontario Provincial Police (OPP) as the residents of these Canadian communities, based on brutal slayings happening almost back-to-back, feared a serial killer might be on the loose.

Another serial killer, one of Canada's most horrific named Robert Pickton, aka "The Pig Farmer Killer," was also killing women at an alarming rate during the same time period. Those atrocities happened near Vancouver, Canada. While police were investigating Pickton, they made numerous pieces of his case public. Canadians, primarily women, were on high-alert. Many women in the region who lived alone, lived in tremendous fear for years. ([3])

A significant backstory into William Fyfe's world actually began in 1979, some twenty years before investigators caught a break and began looking at him as a person of interest in a murder that happened in 1999. Something that has continued to bother me since investigating this case was what did Mr. Fyfe do to pass the time in those twenty years?

I can't imagine the entire time, based on what we know about him, that he was able to plug along in life without committing a single crime. My gut tells me he's responsible for more murders...perhaps many more...and other crimes, but only time, and perhaps science, will confirm this or not.

Numerous unsolved murder cases, more than eighty-five, happened in the Montreal area during the time period of this case (1979-1999). Investigators had hoped they could connect some, or the majority, of the murders to William Fyfe in an effort to close "cold" cases. They were also hopeful to provide the families and friends of the victims some closure. Physical evidence, in a few instances, was obtained but has since been misplaced. Other files did not include physical evidence or leads. William did not confess to any of these unsolved cases, and no physical evidence connected him to them. In this situation, as with many homicides I've investigated, we needed to grasp and consider the past in order to understand what may have caused the present.

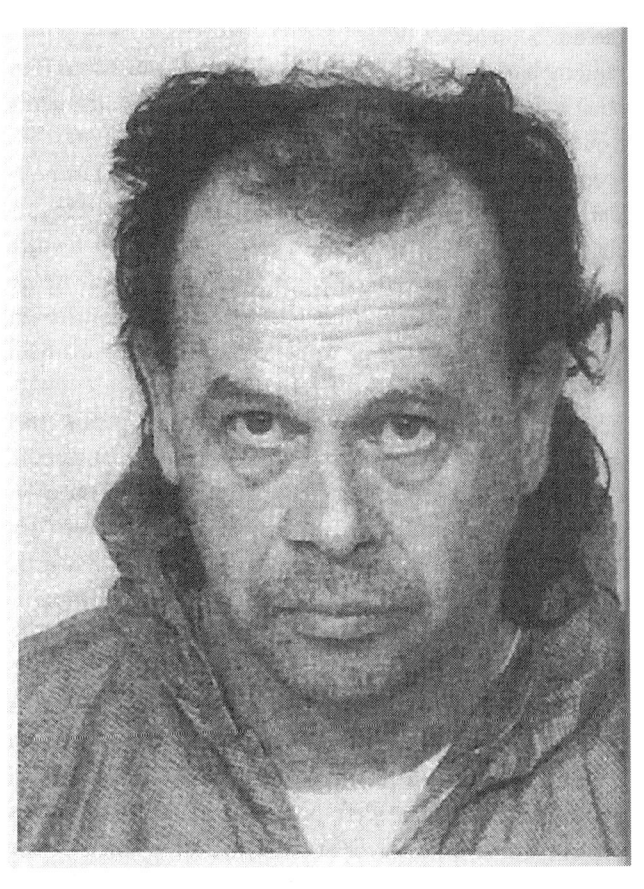

*Canadian Serial Killer
William Patrick Fyfe*

Background

Montreal, Quebec, Canada circa 1979. The city bearing its name from Mount Royal, the triple-peaked hill in the center of the city, and suburbs, was mostly calm. Relocations there were common. Growth was evident, both in technology and agriculture, but not at such a rate to turn people off. Neighbors often knew each other and said, "Hi" when they passed by. Significant community events during that time included the foundation of the Canadian Centre for Architecture and Montreal Holocaust Memorial Centre. Tourists flocked to Montreal too, as they have since, hoping to practice their French and experience the rich cultural life one could find there. Nightlife and high-priced restaurants were available for the chic, and if you wanted to escape the fast-paced life, you could head to the suburbs and chill out. Times were rather good in the late 1970s and early 1980s in Montreal, but someone had come to town who would change all that, basically overnight, ripping the community apart one gruesome murder at a time.

Rumors of a serial killer in Vancouver had made their way to Montreal. However, locals dismissed the stories and were confident nothing like that would happen in their beautiful province. They boasted how safe and clean Montreal was and how proud they were to reside there. Sadly, they had no idea their world was about to be flipped upside down.

A killer, living two very different lives, was graduating from petty crimes to committing cold-blooded murder. William Fyfe was becoming more brazen, more ill-tempered, and his anger had graduated to uncontrollable. Strangely, when he wasn't causing death, fear, and destruction, he was helping people, doing odd jobs for very little money…seeming to genuinely have others' interests in mind. A war raged in his mind, and before long, he would commit some of the most disgusting and filthy crimes I've ever investigated.

Now, let's take a look at the background of this case, which doubles as the backstory of William Fyfe, aka "The Killer Handyman."

Suzanne-Marie Bernier

On October 17, 1979, the corpse of Suzanne-Marie Bernier, a sixty-two-year-old woman, was discovered in Cartierville, Montreal, stabbed several times. Her body, including face and neck, were badly bruised. Further investigation revealed she'd also been sexually violated...after she was dead. Case notes indicated the scene was "gory" and seasoned investigators never recalled seeing such destruction and chaos being done to a human being prior to this. Although the home and scene were scoured for evidence, not much was found. No witnesses came forward and no leads developed. The case remained open but was shelved pending the discovery of new evidence.

Nicole Raymond

On November 14, 1979, the body of twenty-six-year-old Nicole Raymond was discovered in Pointe-Claire, Montreal, stabbed numerous times and brutally beaten. Her remains, as with the case of Bernier, showed signs of sexual assault *after* she was killed. The crime scene, according to accounts relayed by the investigators who were there, was horrific. Blood splatter everywhere and clearly a brutal struggle had ensued prior to Nicole succumbing to her wounds. According to reports, the acts were committed "...by an aggressive animal-like attacker." The authorities who'd investigated Bernier's murder noted similarities at the crime scene for Raymond, but they did not, at that time, believe they were dealing with a serial killer. Again, no witnesses came forward and no concrete physical evidence was obtained to provide investigators with leads. As with the Bernier case, this one also remained on a shelf as a "cold" homicide.

Hazel Scattolon

On March 21, 1981, Hazel Scattolon, a fifty-two-year-old woman, was discovered in Montreal, stabbed numerous times and beaten with a blunt object. A preliminary examination at the scene indicated she had been sexually violated after she died of her wounds. Investigators at this scene recalled the gruesome murders of Bernier and Raymond and noticed similarities to their victim's brutal death. The investigators began to believe the cases were connected based on evidence found at all three crime scenes. Frustrating to them, however, was the fact little physical evidence was obtained at the scene that would help develop a lead or identify a suspect.

After this third murder, the police force began seriously considering a serial killer might be at work. They drew conclusions based on the pattern that had developed: female victims who lived alone, two of the three were in the same age range, they'd been stabbed during an attack with no signs of forced entry. The victims must have willingly let the suspect in, and they'd all been sexually assaulted after they were deceased.

Developing a pattern is one thing, but developing leads and identifying a suspect(s) is generally the hard part. As a previous homicide investigator, I can tell you that this point is among the most frustrating of working these types of cases. You respond to murder scenes, detect a pattern, and then have absolutely no leads to work. I've had many sleepless nights and have worn my teeth down worrying about the victims and my inability to put their family at ease by putting someone in jail for their crime.

Nevertheless, as with the two previous murder cases, this one was shelved and classified as a "cold" case pending the discovery of new evidence or leads.

On September 26, 1987, the body of thirty-seven-year-old Louise Poupart-Leblanc was discovered in Saint-Adèle, Laurentides. Poupart-Leblanc had been stabbed repeatedly. She'd been beaten to death with a blunt object. Further examination of her body revealed she'd been sexually assaulted postmortem. Different than the other cases was the fact that DNA was collected at the scene. Within a few weeks, based on the DNA, it was determined the killer was a male.

General conjecture was that the killer got sloppy while stabbing the victim and had nicked his own hand. Despite their efforts and the wide-spread media coverage for this case, it also went on a shelf as a "cold" case. The DNA was compared to thousands of samples in a database, but no hits surfaced. However, the DNA from this scene would play a significant role twelve years later.

Also, based on the fact Poupart-Leblanc's murder was very similar to the other murders, the investigators began to firmly believe they were trying to identify a serial killer. Instead of wondering *if* another victim would be discovered, the investigators wondered *when* he'd strike again.

Heated meetings at the police department demonstrated the community was beyond scared. Rightfully so. The police department did little to calm their nerves because they did not have answers. Citizens were not convinced the police were acting on everything they could to identify the killer and felt the police were not doing a good job of keeping them safe.

The bottom line is every investigator and police officer I've ever met wants to protect and serve the community. In the case of murder, this testament increases tenfold. We want to catch the killer and will exhaust every possible lead and angle imaginable; however, if there are no witnesses, evidence, or clues left at a scene, we're not magicians.

While reading newspaper articles from the era, I got the sense that law enforcement and the public were completely irate, but for different reasons. The police wanted answers just as badly as the community did, but the truth of the matter was there were no answers to be had. If I were working during that time and assigned to the case, I'd have been stressed out and frustrated too.

The feeling of helplessness, especially for a police officer, is rare but quite difficult to deal with.

As tension mounted in the communities, another tragedy struck. On June 9, 1989, the corpse of Pauline Laplante, a forty-five-year-old woman, was found in Saint-Adèle, Laurentides. Laplante had been stabbed numerous times and beaten to death with a blunt object. Similar to the other four cases, she too showed signs of being sexually violated after she'd been killed. Her murder was the pivotal case in the William Fyfe investigation.

Both the police and the public were convinced a serial killer was stalking and hunting women in the greater Montreal area. Law enforcement officials openly cautioned all women, via press releases, to remain inside and not to answer the door for strangers. Newspapers and radio broadcasts revealed that no sign of forced entry had been found in the five murders and they believed the killer was being let into the homes while playing the part of a handyman or plumber.

Some physical evidence had been located at the latest crime scene, but police were unable to focus on one person. Beyond the fact that the MO was similar and the victim fit the age and description of the other victims, police again had no leads.

It's difficult for me to imagine how helpless the police and community would have felt at this point. You know a serial killer is loose, you know who he's targeting, yet you have no idea who he is or who the next target will be.

Because the killer apparently had worked out a routine and manner in which to gain entry into the victims' homes, this demonstrated a high level of sophistication, which further scared the hell out of the community.

These five murders obviously rocked the various small communities in which they occurred. Police were equally dumbfounded but appeared genuine in wanting to solve the murders. The last thing anyone wanted was widespread confusion and panic, but that's what was happening. Officials were continually asked to provide answers but were unable to do so. They had to admit that they had no solid leads and no positive progress had been made in any of the five murders (stretching over an eight-year period). Rightfully so, the families of the victims were clearly upset and continued to request updates as to what, if anything, the police were doing to catch the killer. Yet, like several homicide cases I've investigated, and despite the efforts of the community and law enforcement to identify a suspect, these homicides went "cold," remained unsolved, and sat on a shelf waiting for some sort of miracle.

The murders stopped abruptly after 1989. Locals and police speculated that perhaps the killer had died, had been killed, or arrested for some other offense and was incarcerated, preventing him from being able to kill more women. Other homicide cases surfaced in Montreal during that time frame, but none of them matched the serial killer's MO.

A majority of the inspectors involved in the first five homicides retired over the next twenty years, but these disgusting, unsolved homicides remained in their minds and in the hearts of the police department personnel who investigated them.

Despite what people may think, homicide investigators become attached to their cases and want to solve them. It takes a special person to work these types of crimes. When you see death, particularly brutal scenes committed by savages, it wears on you. Most homicide investigators at some point ask to rotate out of their position based on the terrible things they see, hear, and process internally.

***

Fast-forward to October 15, 1999, only two days before the anniversary of the Suzanne-Marie Bernier murder that occurred on October 17, 1979. The body of a woman living alone was discovered in her own back yard. She had been killed with a blunt object. Naturally, the case shocked the community, but it was not immediately connected to the murders from twenty years prior.

Nothing unusual about that because investigators work with what is in front of them, then branch out to other cases if they're seeking leads. No one would have guessed at a connection between the cases. At the time, it might have been discussed as a sticking point for citizens as the William Fyfe case moved on, but honestly, to think the police should have known it was the same killer from the murders twenty years prior would be asking far too much. It's very rare for criminals to take a leave of absence from killing, especially twenty years. They almost always get caught in the middle of their killing sprees or end up being killed while police try to apprehend them.

Discussion of a serial killer returning to work did not cross the minds of the investigators, but as they worked the case, several murders followed causing them to reconsider, and later believe that a serial killer was responsible.

Robert, the husband of Anna Yarnold, the female victim in this case, discovered her body (October 15, 1999). At the time, no connection was made with this murder and the previous five discussed here. But, further investigation into Anna's murder, several months later, revealed significant evidence indicating someone completely devoid of human feelings had killed her...and he was not done killing.

Anna, aged fifty-nine at the time of her death, was located in Senneville, Quebec, in her backyard. She'd been beaten with a cement flower pot, located near her head. Whoever had committed the crime then went back into her home and stole items from her purse, indicating the motive for her death was robbery. Puzzling to police, though, was the fact that killing her by repeatedly smashing her head just to steal a few bucks from her purse was extreme overkill. Based on the signs of struggle and destruction inside the home and out, it was obvious Anna had put up a good fight until she perished. Investigators could not wrap their minds around the fact that someone would kill her in such a brutal manner for basically the contents of her purse. They'd later learn that Anna's bank card had also been taken and used. Another small detail that later helped identify the killer.

An article in the Toronto Star stated that people in the tiny Senneville community, population 1,500 were reportedly mortified, "...because crimes like that just don't happen here." Robert Yarnold, Anna's husband, was initially suspected of this heinous crime. The police focused all of their attention on him hoping to solve the murder as quickly as possible. They were focused on trying to put the small community at ease. Unfortunately, the real killer struck again in the next few weeks, further terrifying the town. If you recall what the police did after the fourth murder, you know they began warning people to remain inside, especially women, and not to open their doors for strangers. Immediately after Anna's murder, the police reissued a similar, stern warning: stay inside and don't answer the door for strangers.

Police continued to treat Robert as their main suspect and moved forward with their investigation while listing him as a person of interest in his wife's murder. This was later admitted by the police to be a mistake and caused a delay in locating the real perpetrator. However, this mistake was not the reason the killer was able to kill again. The fact of the matter was there were no other leads, no evidence, and no witnesses for police to interview or follow up with.

On October 29, 1999, the body of forty-five-year-old Monique Gaudreau was found by her sister. Murdered in Sainte-Agathe-des-Monts, Quebec, Gaudreau had been beaten and stabbed several times. Signs of sexual assault added to the clues. Soon it became evident to investigators, after learning from the coroner that Gaudreau had been stabbed approximately fifty-five times, that the person responsible for the murder was obviously angry, clearly messed up in the head, and extremely disturbed. Pools of blood were found throughout her room, and the brutality and manner of her death shocked even the most hardened investigators. While the police and forensic specialists aggressively investigated this case, they still did not identify a suspect right away. Determined to crack the case, police worked throughout the night and into the next morning trying to locate evidence. They were no closer to identifying a suspect when further disaster ensued a few weeks later.

Theresa Shanahan

On November 19, 1999, Theresa Shanahan, fifty-five years old, became the next case. Located in Laval, Quebec, she, like Gaudreau, had been stabbed to death, outrageously at least thirty-two times in addition to being beaten. Investigators noticed the scene was very similar to what they had discovered at Monique Gaudreau's home. Law enforcement began to consider, based on the MO, that there might be a serial killer at work.

The community as a whole expressed outrage. Fear skyrocketed. Average citizens turned to the police for reassurance but did not get it right away. Unbeknownst to the public was the fact that significant evidence was being collected at the scene and local investigators were already chasing leads to identify and apprehend the killer. As police began to piece together Ms. Shanahan's murder case, the shameless killer struck again.

On December 15, 1999, the body of a fifty-year-old woman, Mary Glen, was found. Discovered in Baie-d'Urfé, Quebec, Glen had been beaten and stabbed numerous times, and her body showed signs of sexual abuse. A blunt object was used in addition to her being stabbed. Ms. Glen died a violent death. The crime scene was similar to the previous two (Shanahan and Gaudreau). Police now had four vile murders occurring in less than three months, three of which appeared more than likely done by the same killer.

A wave of panic washed over Montreal. People wanted to hear everything would be all right, but the police were being tight-lipped about their evidence because they did not want to let the killer know they were making progress. Residents demanded updates, but the authorities were slow to release them. Law enforcement wanted to put the public at ease, but their larger obligation meant catching a killer to bring justice to the victims and their families.

This, thankfully, was the last murder the serial killer would commit. Careful comparison of evidence, by the way of a partial smudged fingerprint, located at Ms. Glen's home, would finally provide the investigators a solid lead. Within the halls of the police department, a small roar of cheers could be heard as a person of interest for the murder of Ms. Glen was identified based on fingerprint evidence found at her home. Now, after months of concern, speculation, and frustration, law enforcement finally had someone to investigate...forty-four-year-old William Fyfe.

He was not arrested right away as most people would have expected. That fact served as a source of frustration to community members, but it was clearly the right call. Remember, at the time, he was only a person of interest in one murder, not a suspect. The possibility existed that they could locate William and he would have a logical explanation for his fingerprint being at the murder scene. Ms. Glen could have easily hired him months or even years earlier to do some handyman work around the house. Approaching him right away and confronting him with their evidence could have also spooked him and caused him to run. Either way, if they pushed the investigation too fast, it might have ended up stalled and the investigators would have been back to square one.

Based on evidence police had at the time, William was labeled a "person of interest" for the murder of Ms. Glen, which was why he was not arrested immediately.

The police department, who'd essentially lost all support from the community, actually made a splendid move. Law enforcement was publicly abused during this case but ultimately ended up making several good calls that would prove crucial in the apprehension of William Fyfe, the collection of evidence and a confession from him solving five additional homicides.

Holding information obtained during a murder case is always a judgment call. Right or wrong, it's done in every homicide case because there's an art in identifying suspects, gathering enough evidence for a solid case, and then planning an operation to apprehend them. Similar to a dicey poker game, an experienced homicide investigator never plays all his cards right away. Sometimes holding leads tight to the chest will backfire, but the majority of the time it works to the benefit of the case and the investigator. Unless you've actually worn a badge and worked homicide cases, you'll never understand the tremendous amount of pressure and grief we've experienced. Ultimately, we want the same thing the public wants.

After identifying their person of interest, the Montreal Police Services (MPS) contacted the Ontario Provincial Police (OPP) regarding evidence and William Fyfe. Preliminary information suggested William was staying in Ontario, the purpose for the joint mission. The OPP and MP assembled a team to investigate the four Montreal murders with the focus squarely on William Fyfe. Homicide investigators were intelligent enough to recognize the case required delicate handling while moving forward. Their main task involved determining whether Fyfe was more than a person of interest and if he was responsible for the other three murders. If so, they'd need to develop enough probable cause to secure an arrest warrant for him, and lastly, they'd need to locate and arrest him.

This is a difficult time during a murder investigation. Stress levels jump high, excitement pushes investigators to work long hours, but it's also a dangerous time. Many times cases get botched at this point, and killers end up walking based on mistakes or shoddy investigation techniques.

Although the community and the two police departments were on edge, the fact a strong lead - the fingerprint - had been developed re-energized the case. Every day that passed without a suspect or arrest continued to frustrate the community, but progress behind the scenes was being made.

In fact, William Fyfe would later be followed and apprehended. Let's take a look at the crimes he committed in greater detail before discussing how he was apprehended.

The Crimes

With respect to my research on the cases of Nicole Raymond, Hazel Scattolon, Suzanne-Marie Bernier, Louise Poupart-Leblanc, and Pauline Laplante, not much content was available that accurately depicted the full details of these terrible crimes, at least much more than I've already shared above. I learned that physical evidence had been collected at the scenes in the form of DNA, but the DNA database at the time was small because not many samples had been collected during the 1970s. DNA from the scenes was tested, but no match was made, so the evidence remained booked and did not provide any leads. No witnesses came forward for these five murders, and no further evidence or leads surfaced over the course of twenty years. Such a long period of time had passed that many people, including the families of the victims and law enforcement, believed the cases would never be solved.

Unfortunately, the circumstances of these five murders serves as a reminder to one of the general public's complaints when it comes to law enforcement handling "cold" murder cases. "Cold" cases collect dust because resources and leads are scarce; however, if someone confesses to the killings, and the confession is deemed reliable, the murder investigation will be re-opened. If evidence exists that can validate a confession from the suspect, the suspect is normally charged with the murder. This is how it's done in the United States.

In the case of William Fyfe, he later gave a chilling description of how he committed these five murders. The accurate details he described, and later his DNA located at some of the crime scenes, confirmed William Fyfe did, in fact, kill these women. However, he confessed to those murders *after* the court case concluded for the four murders. Therefore, he was credited with the killings but was not charged with first-degree murder because it didn't matter according to the Crown. He could kill one or a thousand people and receive the same amount of punishment. This type of a loophole in Canadian law would drive me nuts. I'd have to shy away from being a homicide investigator in Canada because I would not deal well with a perpetrator not being punished for taking five human lives.

The focus for the remainder of this investigation revolves around the four murders that occurred between October and December of 1999. Let me paint you a picture of when the case of William Fyfe finally took shape for local law enforcement. It won't be pretty, but it's accurate and real.

Anna Yarnold

Senneville, Quebec, is a tiny, yet tight-knit community located on Montreal's West Island. The area is extremely quiet and any mention of a serious crime, or much crime at all, is non-existent. It's October, and the persistent cold winds have pushed fallen leaves along their merry way. Substantial homes dot the waterfront and are sprinkled inland. Life is good and time cruises by. Residents, most of them living in the area for quite a while, know each other well. They watch each other's kids grow and look out for one another. People are out and about walking their dogs. Children play catch or tag in the streets before it gets too cold and the snow begins to fall.

Approximately three o'clock in the afternoon on October 14, 1999, fifty-nine-year-old Anna Yarnold, a longtime resident and well-respected member of the community, was frantically heading to the veterinarian with her beloved dog, Trooper. She'd discovered a lump on Trooper and was concerned about the dog's well-being. The vet examined Trooper and concluded the lump was dangerous and needed to be removed as soon as possible. Unfortunately, the cost was high and the procedure could be problematic. Upset about the sad news, Anna returned home, contemplating what to do next for Trooper. She wanted the best for her faithful pup.

At 5:30, Anna's daughter Sarah called to check on her mom and asked about Trooper's status. Sarah later recalled that she had told her mother everything would be okay with Trooper, and they'd be fine. Sarah had no idea what was about to happen to her mother.

The next morning, Sarah and her father, Robert, who did not live with his wife, began calling to check on Anna and Trooper. When Anna didn't answer or return their calls, the family began to worry. Anna had always enjoyed sharing news about everyday life with her family, so it was bizarre that she hadn't returned their calls.

Late in the evening, Robert decided to check on his wife's well-being and drove to her home. When he arrived, he noticed the car in the driveway, and he knocked on the door. No answer. Eventually, he entered the home and noticed right away that her dog, Trooper, had not greeted him. That was strange and caused him to search the home. Robert located Trooper hiding behind a bedroom door upstairs, but he still hadn't found his wife. While heading to the backyard, he called out her name and stopped dead in his tracks. Anna lay in a pool of her own blood, her skull caved in and a cement flower pot (later identified as the murder weapon) next to her head. Once the shock of the scene wore off, Robert called the police. His wife, one of the few people he cherished in life, had died a violent death. He was beside himself with grief.

Numerous police and investigators responded to Anna's home. Within minutes, once they completed their initial walk-through, they determined Anna's death had likely been caused during a robbery. Initial reports noted no forced entry, but a struggle had ensued in her bathroom. Anna's glasses were found in the bathroom sink. They believe she had temporarily escaped her attacker, who held her by her hair. Clumps of her hair were found in the bathroom and near the kitchen. Anna fled to the backyard, where she apparently tripped and fell while running for her life. The attacker jumped on top of her, choked her and punched her repeatedly in the face (based on the bruising). Then he grabbed the nearby concrete flower pot and struck her over the head repeatedly. Blunt force trauma took Anna's life.

After the killer murdered her, he went back inside the house, rifled through her purse in her bedroom upstairs, and took some items including her bank card. Details of the homicide were gruesome and even surprising to the investigators. The killer then exited the house and walked away without anyone reporting his heinous acts.

Robert was taken to the police station and questioned at length. The investigators believed him to be the primary suspect in Anna's death. Therefore, they did not initially spend any more time looking for other possible suspects. Eventually, his daughter, Sarah, was asked to report to the police station where her dad was being questioned. No one had told her about the murder. Sarah was asked about her parents' relationship and their family life. Someone finally blurted out the reason for the interrogation. "Well, your mother is dead." The poor handling of her notification remained an issue with Sarah for many years. She should have been told immediately that her mother was murdered, and the police should not have treated her like a suspect.

Sarah and her father remained at the police station for many hours providing statements. When they were both allowed to leave, Robert was asked to stay in town. The case was not highly publicized in the news initially, but it came out the following morning and caused understandable concern. The police would have loved to have had DNA or a fingerprint from the flower pot used to kill Anna, but obtaining that kind of evidence from a cement object wasn't possible, especially if the killer wore gloves. Frustration mounted within the police department because they wanted answers as badly as the public. At that point, they had nothing to work with. The investigation continued, although no new evidence had been discovered, and there were no additional leads for the police to follow.

Monique Gaudreau

Sainte-Agathe-des-Monts, Quebec. Late in October of 1999, residents of the town, bordered by Lake Lac des Sables, prepared for winter. Picturesque and trendy, it is located a hundred kilometers north of Montreal. Because of the opportunities for year-round fun, it grew as a tourist destination. The economy had grown along with the influx of tourists, and the area offered amenities such as boating, fishing, and horseback riding in the summer and winter activities like dogsled racing, skating, and ice hockey. Locals knew each other well and embraced the visitors because tourism helped their town grow.

At 10:25 on the morning of October 29, 1999, people who worked with Monique Gaudreau, a nurse at a local hospital, began to be concerned. She had not shown up to work, a highly unusual situation for her since she enjoyed her job and was normally punctual. Phone calls were made, but no one had seen or heard from her since the end of shift on the previous day. Co-workers took the next step and called Monique's sister to see if she knew where Monique was. They were concerned something was not right and became increasingly so because Monique's sister also had not heard from her.

During a phone conversation on the previous night, Monique had actually mentioned to her sister that she would be at work the following day. Hoping to find out her sister's status, she drove to Monique's apartment and let herself in with the the extra key she had. The apartment checked out clear until she reached the bedroom. Monique's brutally battered body was sprawled at the foot of her bed. Blood still dripped from the wall nearby her sister's lifeless body. Monique's torso and head were mutilated, her clothes had been pulled off around her waist, and she'd been stabbed numerous times.

Stunned, Monique's sister called the police, who arrived immediately. A forensic biologist with law enforcement, Jacinthe Prevost, showed up, along with Montreal Police Services Commander, Andre Bouchard. Prevost found the scene and apparent struggle to be overwhelmingly destructive. She counted approximately fifty-five stab wounds to Monique. Prevost and Bouchard were equally concerned that the carnage was not the work of an average murderer. The perpetrator of this horrendous crime had surely been a sick individual who killed in a fit of rage. Images in that room stuck with all who had been at the scene for the rest of their lives. Prevost also mentioned that it appeared Monique had been sexually violated after she died. That thought sent a chill throughout the law enforcement community.

Notes in the file indicated no forced entry, no fingerprints, and the murder weapon was not left at the scene. If I were to arrive and investigate a similar scene, I'd have been dejected and flat out angry. Someone would have to talk me off the ledge. The public can't imagine the frustration that consumes investigators and those close to the case in these situations. Witnessing and studying a scene where a person has been savagely killed right in front of you, takes a toll on everyone concerned. Police and forensics experts consider the victim and their families. Having no clues, nothing to work with, would have bothered me to no end.

After the scene had been secured and dusted for clues, additional information surfaced, revealing several significant pieces of information pertaining to the murder.

In the landing area near the front door entrance to the home, a bloody shoe print was discovered. This had to be from the suspect because it was in Monique's blood. Secondly, police discovered blood droplets from the front door of the home leading toward the side of the house, likely the route the killer took when fleeing the scene. The investigators surmised that while the suspect stabbed Monique in pure rage, he also cut himself in the process. Initial tests confirmed the blood belonged to a male.

While the police and forensic staff aggressively investigated this murder, they still had no idea whether it was linked to Anna Yarnold's case because Yarnold was not stabbed or sexually assaulted like Monique had been. As they tore apart the crime scene looking for leads, further disaster struck in another nearby community.

Theresa Shanahan

Laval, Quebec. In November of 1999, the largest suburb of Montreal, separated from the mainland to the north by the Rivière des Mille Îles, and from the Island of Montreal to the south by the Rivière des Prairies, became fully immersed in winter. The area, well-known for technology centered on pharmaceutical, industrial, and retail sectors, boasted four significant industrial park centers. Among the most famous attractions in Laval was the Cosmodome, a location featuring both Space Camp Canada and the Space Science Center, which opened to the public in December of 1994. Tourists and those seeking to be involved in the technological boom poured into the community, forming a unique atmosphere.

About ten o'clock that morning, workers at a local firm became puzzled at the absence of their accountant, fifty-five-year-old Theresa Shanahan. Shanahan's co-workers had phoned her home numerous times, to no avail. One of them later told police of their concerns and asked if they could meet at Theresa's home to check on her. When the police arrived, three or four local newspapers were stacked at the front door. Apparently, Theresa had either taken a trip or hadn't left the apartment for a few days. The police officer convinced the building concierge to open the door to Shanahan's apartment. When they all entered, sadly, they located her body lying in bed in a large pool of blood. The scene was too much, even for the officer, who backed out and called for back-up.

Joining the additional staff and police investigators who arrived was biologist, Jacinthe Prevost. Upon entering the scene, she immediately noted similarities between it and the crime scene at Monique Gaudreau's home. Theresa had been sexually assaulted and stabbed numerous times. Prevost's initial assessment concluded that Theresa had been stabbed approximately thirty-two times. The extreme brutality of the scene convinced Prevost and local law enforcement that the person responsible for her murder was likely the same one who'd killed Monique Gaudreau. That observation fueled speculation heard at the police departments and in the public...a serial killer was preying on women in the Montreal area.

Unique to this crime scene was the fact the killer stole Theresa's jewelry and bank cards. This again made the investigators believe Theresa's murder had been senselessly committed during a robbery. As the scene was being processed, that evening and into the next few days, police were notified that Theresa's bank card had been used the night before to withdraw five hundred dollars prior to midnight and another five hundred just after midnight. At the time, it was the daily limit for cash withdrawal at ATMs. The killer, aware of the restriction, had waited until close to midnight to wipe out Theresa's bank account. Law enforcement responded to the bank where Theresa's card had been used and obtained a grainy photograph of the suspect.

The image depicted was clearly a man wearing a hooded sweatshirt, making it impossible to identify him. Exhibiting no visible distinguishing marks, the suspect appeared medium build, approximately five feet ten inches tall. It was also noted that the killer had to know Theresa's PIN number to access her account. He either knew her or had tortured her to get the information before killing her. If this were merely a robbery attempt, why would the killer murder Theresa after she had given him her PIN number?

Around the same time of this investigation, Sarah, the daughter of Anna Yarnold, noticed her mother's bank card had also been used after her death. She alerted the police who quickly obtained photos from the cash machine where Anna's card had been used. They found a similar image of an adult male wearing a hooded sweatshirt. The public anticipated the release of the photo, but when it was released, most people were frustrated because the image showed very little detail. Nevertheless, the investigators were able to determine the suspect was a white male adult, approximately five feet ten inches tall, and at the time of Anna Yarnold's death, he had a beard. This was significant because it was another clue about the identity of the killer, and it ruled out the possibility of Anna's husband, Robert. He'd never worn a beard. Although Robert was eventually ruled out as his wife's killer, officials never apologized for how he'd been treated.

None of the homes demonstrated signs of forced entry, and police believed the suspect had posed as a handyman or plumber and would get the victims to open their doors not knowing what terrible fate they'd succumb to once doing so. This bit of information was provided to the community in an effort to educate citizens about remaining vigilant. But, and rightfully so, this information, coupled with three terrible murders only furthered the public's fear. A serial killer was at work in their areas, and the police were no closer to identifying, let alone apprehending him, than they had been after the first murder. Panic spread like wildfire in the communities around Montreal.

Mary Glen

In Mid-December of 1999, Baie-d'Urfé in Montreal's West Island area was loaded with well-to-do folks associated with private clubs, including the Baie-D'Urfé Curling Club. Residents in this community were among the wealthiest in Montreal, and the homes and surrounding businesses are expansive, modern, and clean. The instances of crime remained very low and morale was high. Baie-D'Urfé has one industrial park, which gobbled up a third of the town's land area, but the location of it was partially hidden from the rest of town. Boutique cafes and local hangout spots were fairly trendy as long as the roads had been cleared of snow. At that time, the ground was covered and residents spent time inside their homes, enjoying cozy fires.

On December 14, 1999, a man knocked on the door of a modest home in Baie-D'Urfé. A woman answered even though she thought it odd a stranger would come to her home. The man explained that he worked as a gardener and asked if she needed any work done. Someone soliciting gardening jobs during December when snow-covered plants would remain covered for months, was strange, to say the least, but she politely turned and summoned her husband. He came to the door and declined his services. The unknown man left the area. Since the woman's husband had been at home, it likely saved her life.

A few minutes later, the same man knocked on the door of a waterfront home in the same community. Mary Glen, a fifty-year-old woman, known for being an outgoing, talented artist, answered the door and turned toward her kitchen after letting the gardener inside. No one knew for sure what ruse the man used to get inside so easily, especially since the pages of local newspapers were covered with the stories of a serial killer being on the loose.

An aggressive and murderous altercation ensued between the man and Mary. The struggle began in the kitchen, moved to an area she used as an office, continued toward the stairs to the first floor of the home, and ended with Mary being beaten to death with a blunt object, stabbed several times, and sexually violated in her kitchen. Evidence was later found in all these areas, including Mary's glasses. Furniture, an art easel, and other household items had been thrown around or knocked over, indicating the fierce confrontation between Mary and her attacker.

After killing Mary, her murderer casually walked to the kitchen sink and washed up. He then went upstairs and into Mary's bedroom where he took items from her purse. The serial killer then left without anyone seeing or hearing anything unusual.

It's common for a true, cold-blooded person to behave in such a manner. To take the time to murder someone, wash blood from your hands in their sink, and then rob them afterward is simply disgusting. I find it puzzling and disturbing that no one heard or saw anything.

The next day, December 15, 1999, a house worker arrived at Mary's home. She knocked on the door, but when no one answered, she let herself in, walked into the kitchen area, and screamed. Mary's completely battered and dead body lay on the floor in a pool of blood. The worker called the police, who arrived quickly. Local authorities also asked noted biologist

Jacinthe Prevost to meet them at the scene. When Prevost arrived, she was stunned to see Mary's murder scene so closely resembled the other two she'd worked. Without a doubt, Prevost and the local law enforcement concluded overwhelmingly that they were looking for a sadistic serial killer. Until he was found and brought to justice, every woman in Montreal was at serious risk.

Faint bloody footprints were discovered inside the home as investigators pieced together the chain of events. Prevost noticed the footprints were different than the ones found at Monique Guadreau's home. The fact they were there, and in the victim's blood, meant they were likely from the killer who'd killed Mary. Very little evidence was collected by police at the scene in the first few hours, but Prevost, the investigators, and forensic photographer, Jean Paul Manier, were adamant there had to be more evidence. The scientist and photographer would not take a break or leave the scene until every piece of vital evidence was collected or documented. Their dedication eventually ended up cracking the case of William Fyfe wide open.

News of the attack and murder of Mary caused a wave of panic to roll through local communities like no one had ever seen. Women no longer left their doors unlocked. Residents refused to answer the door to strangers. Police again cautioned citizens in the Montreal area to be alert. These murders were weighing on everyone. The sadness and frustration for the families of the victims must have been overwhelming.

On the second day of processing the crime scene at Mary's home, forensic photographer Jean Paul made an important discovery. On the door frame just inside her front door, he located a smudged fingerprint and was able to lift it. He returned to his office to work on identifying the person it belonged to. After nonstop dedication, hours and hours of work, he got a match. The fingerprint belonged to forty-four-year-old William Fyfe. A brief but collective sigh of relief traveled throughout the police department as they now had a person of interest in at least three local serial killings.

A great debate ensued about whether or not William Fyfe's name and photograph should be given to the press. On one side of the issue, the police department was concerned that alerting him would cause him to run. The opposing view was that the local community believed the police must reveal that William Fyfe was a person of interest in the case. Finally, it was agreed that police would have a few hours to locate Fyfe before the discovery of his fingerprint at a murder scene went public. Investigators used time wisely and, like many homicide cases I've investigated, they caught a break.

Local police received a tip from one of Fyfe's ex-girlfriends that he might be staying at his mother's secluded home in Barrie, Ontario. The ex-girlfriend also revealed that William was driving a blue Ford Ranger. According to written reports, it was unclear why the ex-girlfriend called the police because, at the time of the call, it was not widely known that William had been identified as a person of interest. Nevertheless, local police handed this information off to the Ontario Provincial Police. Detective Inspector Jim Miller assembled a team tasked with locating William Fyfe.

Jim Miller determined that Fyfe's mother still lived in town (Barrie) and he and his team headed out to the location to find William or the blue Ford Ranger.

They found the home and noted its concealed location down a long, gravel road making it difficult to see people or cars in the area. However, Miller spotted a small blue pickup truck with Quebec plates parked in front of the home. When he ran a check of the registration, it came back to William Fyfe, but with a different address in Montreal. Excitement built between Miller and his team as they believed, based on the tip and the fact a truck registered to him was at the scene, that William Fyfe was in fact in the area. Miller ordered twenty-four hour surveillance at William's mother's home hoping to spot their target. Their intent was to gather more probable cause to arrest him and ensure he could not kill again.

William was observed exiting his mother's home, and he was followed extensively. Investigators from Montreal headed up to Ontario to join the investigation. Police and authorities involved in the case finally had eyes on their person of interest.

It's difficult to describe the feeling of working one of these cases, identifying a suspect, and then seeing him live and in person in front of you. Resisting the urge to jump out and grab him is difficult, but it must be done. Observing what the suspect does sheds light on how they act, which may help build the case against them in the end. Then fear strikes as you don't want to be the one to lose him during the surveillance.

The following day, newspapers across Canada showed a picture of William Fyfe linking him to the murder of Mary Glen. Some papers also suggested a connection to several other recent murders. He'd been observed leaving his mother's home in the blue Ford Ranger and driving to Toronto. While there, surveillance picked him up looking at various newspapers...with headlines listing him as a wanted murder suspect. Fyfe drove back to his mother's home and laid low for about twenty-four hours. It would have been very interesting to be a fly on the wall in that house while a serial killer contemplated his next move.

On December 21, 1999, Fyfe exited his mother's home carrying a black trash bag. He drove into Barrie and was observed circling around to the rear of a local church. He placed the black bag next to bins used to collect items for underprivileged citizens.

After police officers were certain he'd left the area, and while other investigators continued to follow him, someone from the team responded to the location where Fyfe had been seen dropping off the black trash bag. The investigator opened the trash bag and discovered three pairs of running shoes. They each had droplets of blood on them. With this find, the Ontario Provincial Police, specifically Jim Miller, and the Montreal Police believed they had enough physical evidence to convict William Fyfe of at least one murder.

Authorities watched as the suspect was observed pulling into a local filling station, parking next to a gas pump and going inside the convenience store. William exited the store and strolled to his truck as if he'd never done anything wrong and had nothing to hide. Upon opening the driver's door to his truck, investigators from OPP and MP jumped out from their hiding places and apprehended him. He didn't resist and stated, "Why don't you shoot me now?" After the initial spontaneous statement, William shut down and remained quiet for quite some time. He was transported to the OPP station and placed in an interview room where he'd be questioned regarding the murder of Mary Glen.

The interview room had been fitted with a camera and voice recorder. William finally broke his silence when he asked for cigarettes, which he was given. Once taking his first drag from a cigarette, William frowned and became angry. At least three or four times during the interrogation, he yanked the power cords from the camera recording device. William's demeanor was cold. Several times he said, "You guys don't have anything on me." His other remark was, "Call my lawyer." Investigators continued to press him about the fingerprint at Mary Glen's home. He refused to respond. Investigators called for a break and left the room, taking the ashtray containing the used cigarettes Fyfe had placed in it. They now had his DNA. This was a classic move by these investigators. Criminals believe they are more intelligent than everyone else, but oftentimes, they outsmart themselves. The cigarette butts would be crucial for this case and ultimately sealed William's fate.

As he sat in a holding cell, a search warrant was obtained with everything the investigators had collected to date. The judge agreed and signed the search warrant. Local investigators served a search warrant at William's mother's home. His blue Ford Ranger had been included and was also searched. The running shoes he'd left in the bin behind the church in Barrie were sent to the lab for Jacinthe Prevost to examine. Many convincing items of evidence were located in William's truck and at the room he occupied at his mother's home.

Prevost determined almost immediately that the blood on the running shoes was human. Male and female indicators were located on the samples, but they weren't matched to an individual right away. William Fyfe's clothing, seized at his mother's home, also had human blood on them. In total, Prevost examined approximately fifteen items of evidence located in Fyfe's bedroom and truck. These pieces of evidence would significantly impact the case.

Although authorities wanted to interview William further, it was clear he was uncooperative. Therefore, based on what they already knew, and the known evidence at the scene of Mary Glen's home, Fyfe was booked and charged with first-degree murder. The news of a suspect being identified and booked spread quickly throughout Montreal and the rest of Canada. The public was excited and felt more at ease, but no one was happier than the residents on or near West Island.

In the weeks that followed, Jacinthe Prevost worked tirelessly on the pieces of evidence collected by investigators. She put in long hours developing significant probable cause for the investigators, not only in the case of Ms. Glen but other murders William Fyfe was suspected of committing.

The scientist discovered Anna Yarnold's blood on a pair of William's ratty blue jeans taken from the bedroom at his mother's home. That piece alone put him at Anna's murder scene. Prevost also determined the photo from the bank ATM to be a match to William Fyfe. Her blood on his pants and using the stolen bank card from her home clearly made William the prime suspect for her murder.

The running shoes William had thrown away matched the bloody footprints left at Monique's crime scene. Since William had tried to dispose of the shoes, and they were his, it was clear he was connected to Monique's murder too, proving that he was trying to destroy evidence. Blood droplets located at Monique's home were analyzed and compared to William's DNA, gathered from the cigarette butts during his heated interrogation. The blood chemistry was an exact match to William. This irrefutable evidence linked William to another murder.

William's bedroom at his mother's home also held further details. A ring, the same one stolen from Theresa Shanahan's home after she was murdered, was located in a drawer in William's room. Further proof connecting William to Ms. Shanahan's murder would be located later, but he was charged with first-degree murder shortly after the ring had been found during the warrant search. William never said why he had kept the ring...as a trophy or if he'd not located a buyer for it before being apprehended.

With regard to Mary's murder, several items placed William at the scene. First, his fingerprint was located on the door frame of her home. Prevost's lab results also proved another pair of the running shoes matched the bloody footprints located at Mary's home. Lastly, on a shirt located in William's bedroom, Prevost found a small blood droplet. She compared the DNA of the blood and determined it matched Mary's. This evidence sealed the substantial case against William Fyfe.

These facts and confirmed pieces of evidence were presented to the investigators. They were obviously ecstatic. The airtight case they'd been looking for had developed after months of frustration and zero leads. William Fyfe was subsequently charged with the murders of Anna Yarnold, Monique Gaudreau, and Theresa Shanahan. The fact he was charged with the subsequent three murders solidified the public's feeling that the police had, in fact, captured the real serial killer in this case. Only then did residents, particularly women, begin to feel safe in their homes again.

As news spread throughout Montreal and Canada regarding this case, investigators received a call from a young man in Mount Royal who said he'd known William Fyfe twenty years ago. The young man said he played hockey with Fyfe and Fyfe had been hired to paint his mother's home. The caller said his mother, Hazel Scattalon, had been murdered in her home in 1979. He explained that a suspect was never identified in the case, but he was calling the police to see if William Fyfe may have killed his mother.

Investigators checked this significant lead and quickly learned that Hazel Scattalon had been murdered twenty years prior. Her murder was unsolved and had been shelved as a "cold" case. However, investigators at Hazel's crime scene were able to process the DNA. At the time they knew it was for a male, but that was it. Jacinthe Prevost received the evidence sample from Hazel's murder and immediately began processing it. Within a few weeks, she was able to confirm that DNA taken from Hazel's crime scene belonged to William Fyfe.

Jubilation reverberated through the police department because this DNA evidence directly connected William to the murder scene and would be damaging for him in court. William was subsequently charged with Hazel Scattalon's murder based on the tip received from Hazel's son and the DNA evidence linking him to the crime scene.

Shortly thereafter, the court proceedings began for the case against William Fyfe. As far as multiple homicide cases go, this one was fairly quick. ([4]) Much more surprising information was eventually learned about William Fyfe after the court proceedings. Investigators obtained small glimpses into Fyfe's lifestyle and ended up solving several more "cold case" murders.

The Trial

William Fyfe was arrested on December 22, 1999, and charged with the murder of Mary Glen. In the months that followed, DNA evidence and other crucial pieces of physical evidence led investigators to confirm William was the suspect in several murders, for which he would be subsequently charged.

William had an arraignment hearing in January of 2000. He was formally charged with first-degree murder, and although the physical evidence was staggering, he or his attorney originally pled not guilty.

It's not an uncommon ploy used by defense attorneys to stall the case and to make more money for further court appearances. Meanwhile, investigators from three provinces continued searching for more victims. As many as eighty-five "cold" homicide cases which occurred within the twenty years Fyfe was serial killing, are open. Evidence from the crime scenes were compared to William Fyfe's DNA and his MO.

On June 19, 2000, William Fyfe, based on evidence obtained from the crime scenes of the murders of Theresa Shanahan and Hazel Scattolon, was arraigned on two more counts of first-degree murder. (⁵) This development was looked upon highly by the victims' families. It had been a long time coming, but investigators were pleased they could put together a solid case against William.

His preliminary hearing began on November 6, 2000. Jean Lecours, a well-known and aggressive Crown prosecutor, headed up the case. As far as prosecution for a case like this, Lecours was essentially handed the case on a silver platter. It would have been very difficult for a defense attorney to poke holes in it because the investigation was done properly and protocol was followed appropriately. Lecours said he found it "rather troubling" that Fyfe's charges now covered a period of almost twenty years. "It should motivate the police departments and experts to work hard on their investigations" of unsolved murders, said Lecours. Indeed, they did. An overwhelming amount of evidence was collected against William Fyfe but the case still needed to be tried in court.

The prosecution, through primary testimony of Jacinthe Prevost, Jim Miller, Jean Paul Manier, and Montreal Urban Community police Commander André Bouchard, demonstrated without a doubt that the physical evidence against William Fyfe was obtained lawfully and processed according to the accepted practices at the time of the case. Each member of the law enforcement community who testified was sound and provided excellent authentication on behalf of the Crown against William.

In addition, as more evidence for other homicide cases was collected during his court proceedings, investigators requested and received permission to speak to the accused. The practice had previously been taboo since he was in the middle of a murder trial. Court authorities granted the request and allowed William open access to speak to the police. The prisoner hinted at his willingness to discuss details of other alleged homicides. Hoping not to cause a problem down the road, the investigators backed off and waited until the existing case was completed before speaking to him about other suspected murders. Law enforcement did not want to be accused of tampering with the suspect, so they backed off.

On September 21, 2001, William Fyfe stunned the courtroom by changing his plea from not guilty to guilty. (⁶) Sarah, Anna Yarnold's daughter, recalled being in court for one of the hearings and described Fyfe as, "a pathetic little old man who was sick in the head." It was bittersweet for her and the rest of the families of the victims he'd murdered when he pled guilty. The healing process could finally begin, although extremely difficult. His guilty plea was a great success for all the agencies involved in the case, and it marked the beginning of what we would eventually know about William Fyfe.

Once the court case was complete, the families of the victims ultimately reached out to the Montreal Police and the Ontario Provincial Police to thank them. This case, and how it was handled and investigated, prompted many discussions between citizens and law enforcement about how to do things better in the future. Overall, however, based on my examination of the available case details, law enforcement agencies did a fairly good job and should be commended for apprehending one of Canada's worst serial killers.

Sentencing

In Canada, a second-degree murder conviction carries a maximum punishment of a life sentence, with no possibility of parole for a period of ten to twenty-five years. The term is set by the trial judge.

On October 16, 2001, William Fyfe was sentenced to twenty-five years in prison, with no possibility of parole.

I personally hope he never sees light outside a prison wall.

It should be noted that based on Crown Law, he did not receive any extra time for the five murders he later confessed to. In the United States, twenty to twenty-five years, or more, would have been added to a sentence for *each* victim, ensuring the murderer would never leave prison.

On a positive note, change may be on the horizon in Canada as it pertains to sentencing. Prime Minister Stephen Harper has proposed legislation, with significant backing, that would make some crimes, such as those William Fyfe committed, punishable by life in prison with no chance of parole. I openly support such change.

Conclusion

The case of William Fyfe was a significant one for Canada and the people of Montreal. Several developments occurred *after* William Fyfe was apprehended. Authorities learned there was much more to investigate and discuss once he was convicted.

On November 23, 2001, William Fyfe agreed to give an interview to investigators regarding several other homicides they believed he committed. What he was about to say and describe would surprise investigators. Most of those involved were people who thought they'd heard everything during their careers. It came at a cost, however, as William negotiated a prison location change in exchange for his statement.

"He was a vicious murderer," Montreal Urban Community police Commander André Bouchard would later say after interviewing Fyfe on November 23. ([7])

William sat very still in a cold room at the prison and told investigators that he killed his first victim while out on a day pass from a Montreal jail for a minor crime (1979, Nicole Raymond). Describing how he got into his victims' homes, he said he'd ring the doorbell or knock on the front doors in affluent communities, especially west of Montreal. The would-be victims would invite him inside without a care. He provided specific gruesome details of how he killed Raymond, but his confession did not stop there. Before long, William confessed to four additional murders. His statements and the details he provided convinced the police that he was, in fact, guilty of at least five more murders.

"You couldn't invent those details," Commander Bouchard said.

As mentioned, in exchange for this confession, William negotiated a transfer from a Quebec prison, where he was serving a twenty-five-year sentence for multiple murders, to a prison in western Canada.

Investigators believed this was a good deal because they concluded William was serving time regardless of where he was housed. If they could clear some unsolved murder cases, they thought it was a proper exchange. The public did not like the deal, but it went through anyway.

"I don't know the difference between an eight-by-eight-foot cell in western Canada and an eight-by-eight-foot cell in Quebec," Commander Bouchard said. "He got it in English instead of in French, and that's what he asked for."

Marc Labelle, who represented William during his trial and after his incarceration, argued that his client would receive specialized treatment in the other prison which the prison in Quebec did not provide. The Saskatoon facilities offered psychiatric care for inmates of Fyfe's ilk. He also said William was trying to get away because his case in Quebec had been highly publicized. ([8]) His request caught some people off guard because it suggested he fully understood that what he had done was wrong. His attorney said Fyfe was also seeking help to cure his murderous ways. The majority of serial killers do not share similar feelings. They seek popularity and feel what they've done was right and normal.

After the interview, the investigators described William as manipulative and stubborn. He was open about many of the sick things he'd done in his life, but he refused, over the course of three years of interviews, to ever state *why* he killed so viciously. It was noted during the interview that William, unlike most serial killers, was determined to avoid the spotlight, which led Commander Bouchard to believe William understood what he did was wrong. In fact, this interview was not made public until after William had been flown out of town, again demonstrating his wish to avoid celebrity.

"Usually, serial killers love the publicity, and when they're caught, they're all over the place," Commander Bouchard said. But in Mr. Fyfe's case, "even though he's a serial killer, he knew that what he did was wrong."

Troubling to me, as well as every investigator or law enforcement official involved in this case, are the significant gaps in William Fyfe's life that cannot be explained. Also concerning is the fact that William chooses not to disclose what he did during these times. He felt comfortable disclosing the fact he killed five women, but not comfortable enough to fill in time gaps? As mentioned earlier, over eighty-five murder cases remain open in Canada, particularly in the Montreal area. Some of those homicides could be the work of William Fyfe. As such, and based on what we do know of him and how he brutally killed nine women, it's likely the case of William Fyfe will never be officially closed. You can't shelve his file away and honestly think he wasn't responsible for other murders in those twenty years.

Many have speculated that some sort of significant relationship or sexual situation forced William to commit sexual acts with the women he killed. Some psychologists believed he obtained some sort of gratification by having sex with his victims, but in each of the cases he did so, the women were dead or dying at the time. Perhaps the wires in William's mind became crossed or over-taxed during the fights with his victims and eventual chaotic killings of his victims causing him to need a sexual outlet to calm himself. The fact remains, William still refuses to answer about the sexual assaults or his reasons for the murders themselves. It's possible he suffered some sort of mental deterioration due to extensive drug use which caused him to have psychotic episodes. To stab his victims repeatedly then sexually assault them simply to take their money just doesn't add up. He burglarized many of the victims and tortured them for the PIN numbers to their bank cards demonstrating clearly how desperate he was for cash. His murder sprees seemed to occur during winter months when handyman and gardening jobs would be less available, requiring him to seek other means of getting cash.

It's my belief that he needed drugs to function "normally." One can only wonder why not just rob the victims and be done with it once you have their bank cards or jewelry? Until he decides to speak again, we'll likely never know the answers to these questions. He was once asked why he stabbed his victims so many times. He smiled and responded, "That's for me to know." What kind of sick individual talks like that?

Murder cases almost always reveal, at some point, a motive for someone, or, in this case, multiple people, losing their lives. I've seen many associated with money or lovers' quarrels, but the majority did not include sexual assault, especially after the victim was murdered. Unique to this case is the fact, even as of today, William Fyfe has never revealed reasons for any of it. Many have speculated that sometime during his childhood, or early adult stages of development, something happened to Fyfe causing him to snap.

I believe serial killers are exposed to terrible environments and become killers. I don't think anyone is born to kill. Based on my research, the cases I've investigated, and the volumes of data available with regard to serial killers, it seems likely William was exposed to or lived through a truly unthinkable event or series of events that, coupled with extreme drug usage, turned him into one of Canada's worst serial killers.

It's unclear whether or not a motive for William's killing sprees will ever be identified. Unlike most of these people, he's run away from the notoriety of his salacious acts and has not been interested in making money or becoming famous based on his case.

A portion of William Fyfe's case that I briefly mentioned previously is his connection, and suspected identity, to also being the so-called "The Plumber Rapist."

Between 1984 and 1987, after William's fifth murder and years prior to his second killing spree in 1999, several women in the downtown Montreal area began reporting being raped by a man who posed as a plumber. His MO was to knock on the door and tell the female victim that the building owner or manager hired him to inspect the pipes in their apartment. The suspect dressed the part and appeared sincere, so the victims would let him in. Once the door was opened, he would immediately force the women to the floor and rape them.

None of the women were killed, and he did not steal from their homes. Montreal Police, after similarities were drawn between the murders committed by William in 1999 and the serial rapes between 1984 and 1987, believe that perpetrator to be William. However, he was never charged with any of the rapes and never confessed to raping anyone in the downtown Montreal area. The fact William posed as a handyman and knocked on the doors of the victims he would later murder, then sexually assaulted several of them, seems to indicate strongly that William was probably responsible for the rapes between 1984 and 1987. Nevertheless, even if he were linked to these terrible crimes, he'd never receive additional prison time based on Crown Law. Yes, it still blows my mind.

William Fyfe should never step outside a prison or psychiatric ward ever again. Canadian prisons, similar to those in the United States, are not suited for the rehabilitation of serial killers. I personally believe there is no way to rehabilitate a person like William Fyfe, or any serial killer, for that matter. When someone snaps and goes that far away from being civilized, there is no going back to what society defines as "normal." My research, experience, and science confirm this. The mental and physical damage William plagued the community with will never go away. The families of the victims will never completely heal. I continue to be haunted by the unknown of what William did for twenty years, between killing sprees, and hope one day soon he decides to speak about everything he's done. The ball is in his court, but I'd be lying if I didn't admit that I'd sure like to take it from him.

Author's note:

I attempted to interview William Fyfe but was unable to because he's currently in a psychiatric facility and the medical staff would not allow a meeting. One of the main players in this case, Commander Andre Bouchard, with Montreal Police Services, had recently retired and was also unavailable for interview. As such, holes exist in William's life story, primarily from his adolescent years.

About Crimes Canada: True Crimes That Shocked the Nation

This is a multi-volume twenty-four book collection, (one per month, each approximately 100 to 180 pages) project, by crime historian Dr. Peter Vronsky and true crime author and publisher RJ Parker, depicting some of Canada's most notorious criminals.

Crimes Canada: True Crimes that Shocked the Nation will feature a series of Canadian true crime short-read books published by *VP Publications* (Vronsky & Parker), an imprint of *RJ Parker Publishing, Inc.*, one of North America's leading publishers of true crime.

Peter Vronsky is the bestselling author of *Serial Killers: The Method and Madness of Monsters* and *Female Serial Killers: How and Why Women Become Monsters* while RJ Parker is not only a successful publisher but also the author of 18 books, including *Serial Killers Abridged: An Encyclopedia of 100 Serial Killers*, *Parents Who Killed Their Children: Filicide*, and *Serial Killer Groupies*. Both are Canadians and have teamed up to share shocking Canadian true crime cases not only with fellow Canadian readers but with Americans and world readers as well, who will be shocked and horrified by just how evil and sick "nice" Canadians can be when they go bad.

Finally, we invite fellow Canadians, aspiring or established authors, to submit proposals or manuscripts to *VP Publications* at *Editors@CrimesCanada.com*.

VP Publications is a new frontier traditional publisher, offering their published authors a generous royalty agreement payable within three months of publishing and aggressive online marketing support. Unlike many so-called "publishers" that are nothing but vanity presses in disguise, VP Publications does not charge authors in advance for submitting their proposal or manuscripts, nor do we charge authors if we choose to publish their works. We pay you, and pay well.

Thank you to our editor and proof-readers for your support:

-- VP Publications

Bettye McKee

Lorrie Suzanne Phillippe

Marlene Fabregas

Darlene Horn

Ron Steed

June Julie Dechman

Katherine McCarthy

Robyn MacEachern

Mary Daniels

Kim Jackson

Vicky Matson-Carruth

Other Books in Crimes Canada

1. *Robert Pickton: The Pig Farmer Killer* by CL Swinney (March 2015)

2. *Marc Lepine: The Montreal Massacre* by RJ Parker (April 2015)

3. *Paul Bernardo and Karla Homolka: The Ken and Barbie Killers* by Peter Vronsky (May 2015)

4. *Shirley Turner: Doctor, Stalker, Murderer* by Kelly Banaski (June 2015)

5. *Canadian Psycho: The True Story of Luka Magnotta* by Cara Lee Carter (July 2015)

6. *The Country Boy Killer* by JT Hunter (August 2015)

7. *The Killer Handyman* by CL Swinney (September 2015)

8. *Hell's Angels Biker Wars: The Rock Machine Massacres* by RJ Parker (October 2015)

http://www.CrimesCanada.com/

About the Author

Chris Swinney is an active Homicide Detective in the San Francisco Bay area. His writing includes the bestselling *'Bill Dix Detective Series',* which he based the books on his experience as a cop and the first book in Crimes Canada - *'Robert Pickton: The Pig Farmer Killer'*.

Chris is a big time supporter of Teachers, Parents, Law Enforcement, Doctors, Nurses, Firefighters, American Troops, Juvenile

Diabetes Research, and children. He spends time volunteering for his church, at schools, he coaches, and every once in awhile he gets to go fly fishing.

Visit Chris at:

__Publisher's Author Page__

__Amazon's Author Page__

__Google Plus__

__Goodreads__

__Twitter__

__PoliceOne__

__Facebook__

TABLE OF CONTENTS

Introduction 9

Background 27

The Crimes 51

The Trial 87

Sentencing 92

Conclusion 94

Author's note 103

About Crimes Canada: True Crimes That Shocked the Nation 105

Other Books in Crimes Canada 109

About the Author 111

1 http://murderpedia.org/male.F/f/fyfe-william-patrick.htm

2 https://www.youtube.com/watch?v=ZiQhacaErFk

3 Robert Pickton: The Pig Farmer Killer, by Chris Swinney, released March 1, 2015

4 http://www.theglobeandmail.com/news/national/very-very-ordinary-man-one-of-worst-serial-killers/article1034872/

5 The Montreal Gazette. 01/29/2000

6 http://www.cbc.ca/news/canada/fyfe-charged-with-two-more-murders-1.226716

7 http://www.theglobeandmail.com/news/national/very-very-ordinary-man-one-of-worst-serial-killers/article1034872

8 http://en.wikipedia.org/wiki/William_Patrick_Fyfe

Made in the USA
San Bernardino, CA
13 April 2016